Understanding Money

Earning Money

Nick Hunter

Raintree

www.raintreepublishers.co.uk
Visit our website to find out
more information about
Raintree books.

To order:
☎ Phone 0845 6044371
🖶 Fax +44 (0) 1865 312263
🖥 Email myorders@raintreepublishers.co.uk

Customers from outside the UK please telephone +44 1865 312262

Raintree is an imprint of Capstone Global Library Limited,
a company incorporated in England and Wales having its
registered office at 7 Pilgrim Street, London, EC4V 6LB –
Registered company number: 6695582

Edited by Megan Cotugno
Designed by Ryan Frieson
Original illustrations © Capstone Global Library, Ltd.
Illustrated by Planman Technologies
Picture research by Mica Brancic
Originated by Capstone Global Library, Ltd.
Printed and bound in China by Leo Paper Products Ltd.

ISBN 978 1 4062 2169 5 (hardback)
15 14 13 12 11
10 9 8 7 6 5 4 3 2 1

ISBN 978 1 4062 2176 3 (paperback)
16 15 14 13 12
10 9 8 7 6 5 4 3 2 1

British Library Cataloguing in Publication Data

Hunter, Nick.
Earning money. -- (Understanding money)
1. Work--Juvenile literature. 2. Wages--Juvenile
literature. 3. Occupations--Juvenile literature.
I. Title II. Series
331.2'1-dc22

Acknowledgements
The author and publishers are grateful to the following for
permission to reproduce copyright material:

Corbis pp. 4 (Redlink/© Uden Graham), 6 (© Simon Jarratt), 8
(© Sandro Vannini), 10 (© Bettmann), 11 (© Hulton-Deutsch
Collection), 13 (© Rykoff Collection), 14 (© Hulton-Deutsch
Collection), 15 (© Image Source), 17 (In Pictures/© Andy
Aitchison), 18 (JAI/© Jon Arnold), 19 (© Amit Bhargava), 21
(Reuters/© Kimberly White), 23 (© Randy Faris), 26
(© Najlah Feanny), 28 (Jose L. Pelaez/© JLP), 33 (© Jose Fuste
Raga), 42 (dpa/© Susana Gonzalez), 43 (© Rune Hellestad),
35 (© Bettmann), 36 (Golden Pixels LLC/© Pablo Rivera), 40
(Somos Images/© Karin Dreyer), 41 (© Sean Justice); Getty
Images p. 31 (Michael Ochs Archives); Shutterstock pp. 25
(© Lein de León Yong), 39 (© Artifan); The Art Archive pp. 9
(Museo Civico Bologna/Gianni Dagli Orti), 12

Cover photograph of car plant worker on production line
reproduced with permission of Getty Images (Cultura/Monty
Rakusen).

We would like to thank Michael Miller for his invaluable help
in the preparation of this book.

Every effort has been made to contact copyright holders of
any material reproduced in this book. Any omissions will
be rectified in subsequent printings if notice is given to the
publisher.

Contents

You can find the answers to the Solve it! questions on page 45.

Some words are shown in bold, **like this**. You can find out what they mean by looking in the glossary on page 46.

What is the economy?

If you ask someone what the economy is, that person will normally say it is all about money. That is partly true, but it is nowhere near the whole story.

An economy is the total of all the **wealth** created in a society. Wealth does not just mean money. It also includes goods and services that are made by human work. Goods are things that are made, sold, and purchased. Services are things that one person pays another person to do. Most goods and services we use or need are created by work. Food is grown and then prepared for us to eat. Machines like cars are made in a factory. Even music is created by the work of a musician.

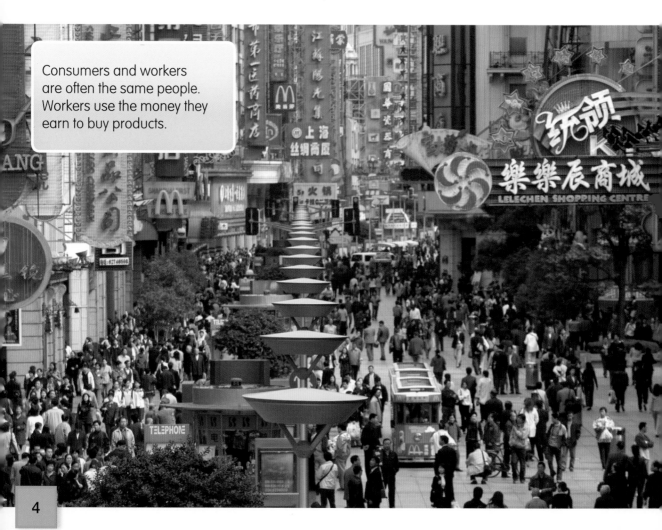

Consumers and workers are often the same people. Workers use the money they earn to buy products.

Sometimes we talk about the world economy, which includes all the wealth created in the world. We might also talk about the economy of our own country, which is linked to the world economy in many ways. You could even think of each household as a small economy.

Parts of an economy

There are three key parts of an economy that we need to understand:

- **Consumers**: These are the people who buy and use goods and services to meet their needs, whether those are basic needs such as food, or luxuries like the latest designer clothes. We are all consumers.

- Workers: These are the people who make the products the consumers need. They usually get paid money in return for their work.

- Business owners or **capitalists**: These are the people who own businesses and employ workers. They **invest** money in order to make more money, or **profit**.

Our economy is called a capitalist economy. This illustration shows the links between owners, workers and consumers. Other key parts of the economy are banks and governments.

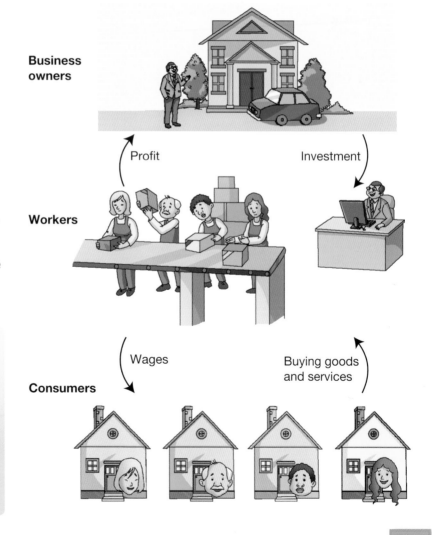

5

Why do people need to earn money?

If you get pocket money or earn money yourself, you use that money to buy things. You might choose to buy things for yourself or presents for your friends. If you did not have that money, you would not be able to buy anything.

Most of the things we need to live our lives cost money. Some goods and services are essential, or necessary for life. Each family has to buy food and drinks. Electricity and water bills need to be paid. People need to earn money to pay for these things that they need to live.

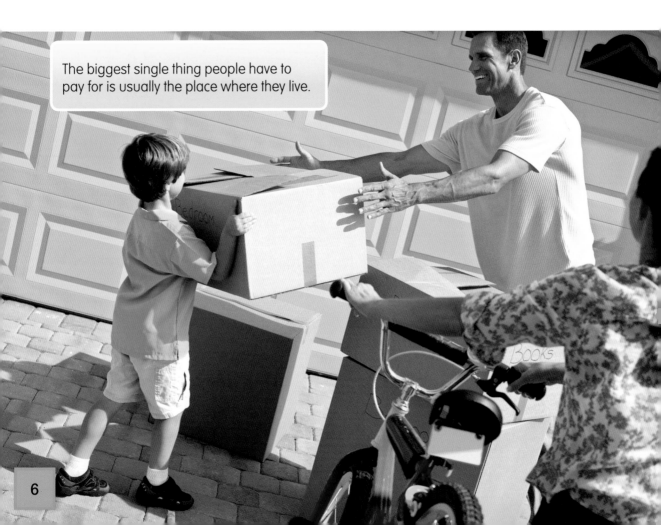

The biggest single thing people have to pay for is usually the place where they live.

Other things are not quite so important. Some of us like to buy new clothes, the latest mobile phone, or to go on holiday. Whether we can afford to buy all the things we want depends on how much money we earn. Most of us have to make choices about which things are most important to spend our money on.

Paying taxes

Other services we use, like roads and schools, also cost money to build and run. We do not normally pay for these directly. Some of the money we earn goes to the government to pay for these essential public services. This money is called tax.

Solve it!

Your budget

The amount of money you have to spend is your **budget**. Make a list of what you spend each week on different things. What are the essential items and what are the things that you could do without?

MY WEEKLY BUDGET

Income

Pocket money	£3
Money from washing cars	£5
Total income	£8

Fixed expenses

Mobile phone costs	£2.50
Savings	£2

Other expenses

Snacks and drinks	£2
Magazines	£1.50
Total spending	£7.50

Has the way that people earn money changed?

In the earliest times, people would hunt animals and gather wild plants to provide for their basic needs. Once humans learned how to grow crops, a system of exchanges, or **barter**, started. Hunters would exchange the animals they caught for crops grown by the farmers. As societies became more complex and more goods were bartered, this system did not work as well. Societies began to develop money as something that everyone could recognise as having **value** (worth) for exchanges.

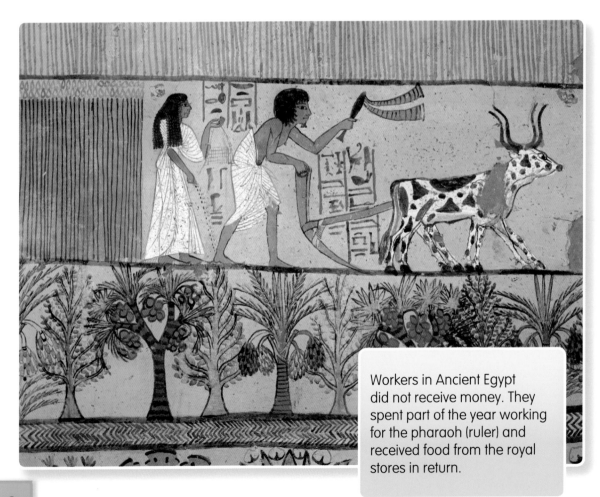

Workers in Ancient Egypt did not receive money. They spent part of the year working for the pharaoh (ruler) and received food from the royal stores in return.

Earning money in ancient times

In ancient civilizations, most people were not **employed** by someone else who paid them money in return for their work. Most people worked for themselves and sold what they produced to earn money. This was true whether they were a farmer growing wheat and selling it, or a baker who bought the wheat, made bread, and sold it. Businesses that required a large number of workers would often use **slaves**, who were bought and sold, rather than paying people to work for them.

In societies like Ancient Greece and Rome, many people lived in cities. Specialist jobs started to develop, such as craftspeople making fine clothes and jewellery. During the **medieval** period, these craftspeople were organized into official **guilds** to ensure quality work and to protect their rights.

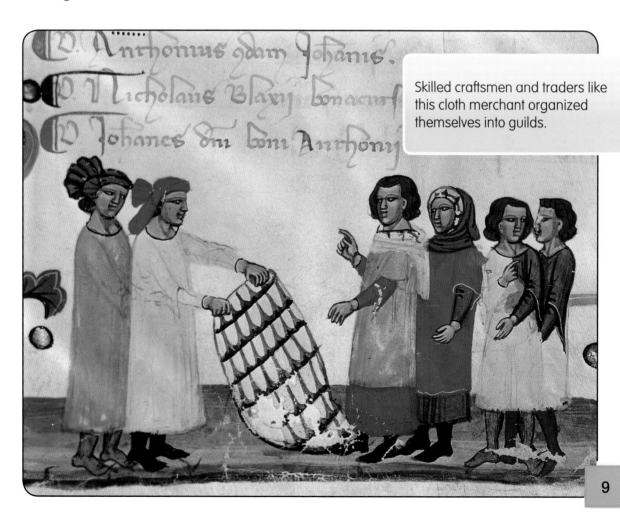

Skilled craftsmen and traders like this cloth merchant organized themselves into guilds.

The feudal system

In medieval Europe, many people outside the cities farmed land that was owned by the local lord. A proportion, or part, of the crops they grew was given to the lord. The lord could sell these crops to earn money and pay for things, such as building castles and fighting wars. In return, the lord would protect the people who farmed the land. This was called the **feudal system**.

Over time, farming methods improved. This meant that fewer people had to work on the land and more food was produced that could be sold. This led to new ways of earning money, too. New **industries** began to develop.

Merchants and trade

New inventions also changed how money could be earned. Ships could sail to far off lands to find goods like pepper and spices. **Merchants** could make a lot of money selling these goods, but it was risky. If the ship was lost at sea, they could lose everything.

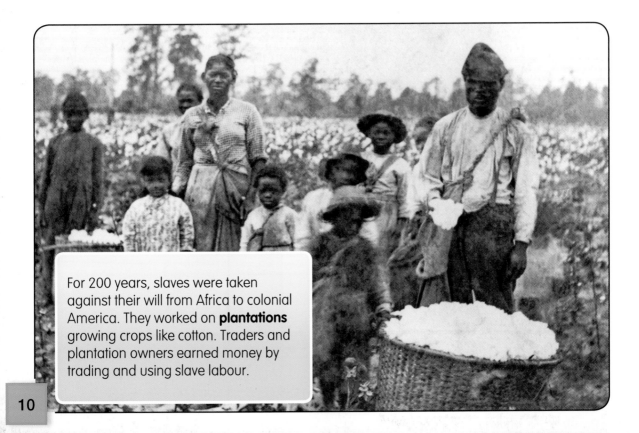

For 200 years, slaves were taken against their will from Africa to colonial America. They worked on **plantations** growing crops like cotton. Traders and plantation owners earned money by trading and using slave labour.

Adam Smith (1723–1790)

Adam Smith was born in Kirkcaldy, Scotland. His book *The Wealth of Nations* (1776) included many new ideas about earning money and the world of work. He worked out that large factories could produce more goods than small workshops. If the tasks involved in making something were each done by different workers, this would produce more than if each worker was doing all the tasks involved. Smith's ideas about how work should be organized were the basis for how we earn money today.

Factories changed where people lived, as well as how they earned money. New cities grew up around the new factories.

Industrial Revolution

From the mid-1700s, major changes took place in the way people earned money. This time of change was called the **Industrial Revolution**. It happened first in Britain, followed by other European countries, North America, and Japan. New technologies, such as steam power, and powerful machines for spinning and weaving cloth meant that many more goods could be produced more quickly.

To use these new machines, people had to work in large factories. Setting up these factories and paying the workers required large amounts of money, or capital. This was the start of the **capitalist** system we have today.

The first industrial workers worked long hours in dangerous and dirty conditions. They would often work seven days a week. Over time, laws were introduced to protect workers and stop employers from using children as workers.

Moving to cities

Even after the Industrial Revolution, not everyone earned money by owning or working in factories. When people moved to towns and cities to work in the new industries, it created many other new jobs. These new communities of workers and owners needed shopkeepers, bakers and even lawyers to supply thier needs.

Henry Ford (1863–1897)

Henry Ford built his first car in Detroit, Michigan, in 1896. His **assembly line** system was designed to mass produce cars like the Ford Model T. Each worker would fit one part of the car as it moved along the assembly line. This produced many more cars than if each worker was producing a whole car alone. This mass production meant that the Ford Model T could be produced cheaply enough to be bought by ordinary families.

An Assembly Line
of the
Ford Motor Company

What has changed since 1900?

Nowadays, most women work outside the home in paid jobs. This was not the case in 1900, although more women were starting to earn money. The number of women working increased when many men went to fight in World War I between 1914 and 1918.

Changes in technology since 1900 have meant that fewer people work in factories today. Many factories also became cleaner and safer. New products, such as computers are made in different ways and conditions, compared to the products of the **Industrial Revolution**.

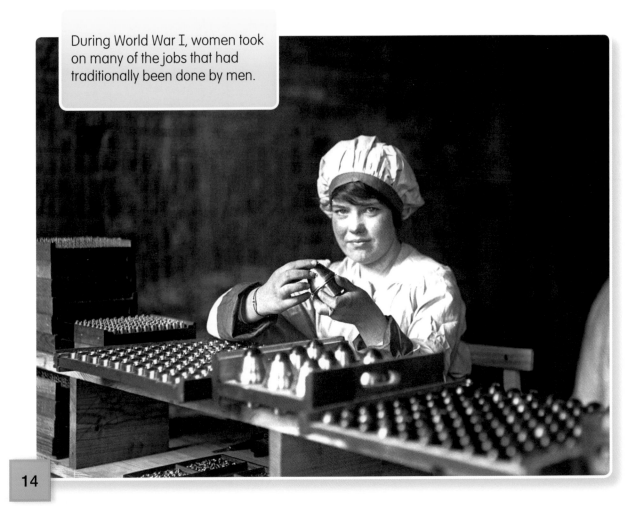

During World War I, women took on many of the jobs that had traditionally been done by men.

Globalization

Since the late 1900s, work and earning money has changed because of **globalization**. Different parts of the world have become more closely connected than in the past. This is because of the growth of instant communication through the phone and internet. Air travel means that people and goods can move around the world more quickly. Many of the products that are bought in North America and Europe are now made in Asia and shipped to customers around the world.

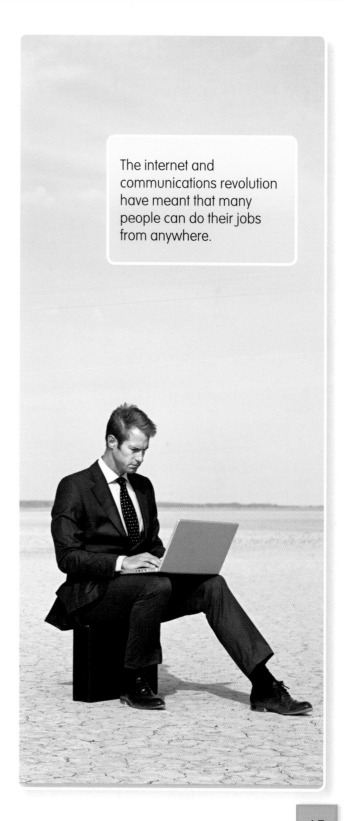

The internet and communications revolution have meant that many people can do their jobs from anywhere.

Larry Page and Sergey Brin
founders of Google

The Google search engine is used by millions of people around the world to find information. Larry Page and Sergey Brin came up with the idea for the search engine while they were students. The company was founded in 1998 and its two founders are now billionaires.

How do people earn money now?

Most people earn money by working for an individual or a corporation. They are paid for the work they do. The jobs that people do are normally divided into two main areas:

- Work that uses **natural resources** to create products that can be exchanged for money. This group can be divided into agricultural workers who grow food and other materials, and industrial workers who use **raw materials**, such as iron, to make products.

- Work that provides services to others, including teachers and firefighters. These workers do not make a product, but they provide services that, in many cases, we could not live without.

Agriculture and farming

All our food has to be grown and harvested from the world around us. The breakfast cereal you ate this morning was made from crops grown on a farm. Animals for meat also have to be fed and looked after on farms. Farmers earn money by selling the things they farm. Some may be sold directly to supermarkets; others will be sold to companies to be processed into food.

Improved farming methods and technology mean that only around two per cent of workers in North America and Europe work in **agriculture**. In poorer countries, many more people are farmers, but many of these farmers only grow food or keep animals to feed themselves and their families.

Fair trade coffee

Many consumers try to buy things as cheaply as they can. Supermarkets and food companies try to pay as little as possible to the farmers that grow the product. Many farmers in **developing countries** are very poor and earn little money from their crops. If you buy products, such as coffee that are marked as **"fair trade"**, this means that the farmers have earned more money for their crop. These products often cost more, but **consumers** know that the farmers earn a larger share of the money they pay.

Working in industry

Industry means turning raw materials into useful products. This ranges from mining minerals, such as coal, to the materials used for making highly complex products, such as an aircraft. Building workers earn money building houses and other structures, such offices and roads.

Manufacturing

Most people who work in industry earn money by making the products that we use every day. This is called manufacturing. The **Industrial Revolution** led to people working in large factories, and many still do, but some manufacturing is done by highly skilled people in small workshops. Manufacturing workers may make finished products or parts that will be included in a bigger product, such as a car.

Many of the products we buy are made thousands of miles away. These clothes may have been made in China, where workers earn less money. This means that the clothes can be made more cheaply.

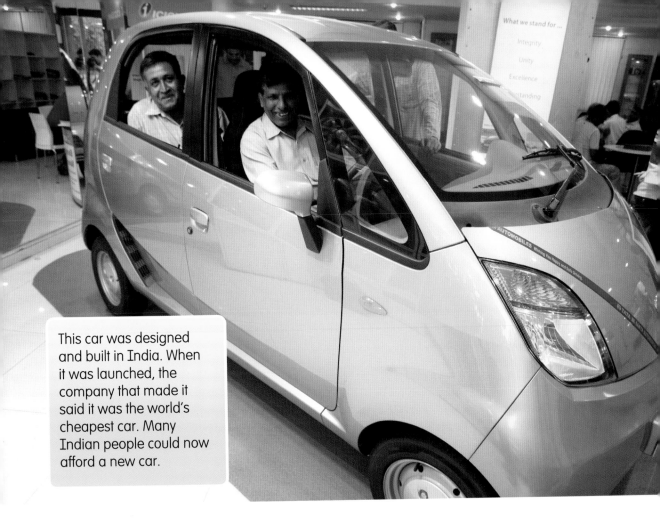

This car was designed and built in India. When it was launched, the company that made it said it was the world's cheapest car. Many Indian people could now afford a new car.

The motor industry

Industries change when technology develops and people want to buy different things. The city of Detroit, Michigan, was called "the motor city" because so many cars were made there by Ford, General Motors, and Chrysler. Since the 1970s, this industry has declined as people bought cars from other countries. These cars were cheaper and used less fuel. This means that many workers who earned money in the car-manufacturing industry in Detroit have had to find work elsewhere.

Manufacturing is not the only area of industry. Many people work to convert, or change, raw materials into things that we use every day. They are things that we barely notice until they are not there. If you have ever been in a power cut, you know how different life can be without utilities such as electricity, gas, and water. Many people earn money making sure these essential services reach us, and by mining raw materials, such as coal and oil to provide us with energy.

High-tech industry

Some of the products made by people who work in industry have not changed for centuries. But products such as computers, mobile phones, and other gadgets are changing all the time. As well as making the products themselves, people are **employed** to design new models. There are also big teams of people whose job it is to **advertise** new products to consumers and make sure the products reach the stores where they will be sold. They all earn money from the company that makes the product.

Who made my MP3 player?

Your MP3 player may carry the name of a well-known company, such as Sony or Apple. You would think that it was made in Japan or the United States. The people who invented, designed, and sold the product may be in one of these countries, but the parts were probably put together in a huge factory in China. The many different tiny parts that make up one MP3 player were made in different factories around the world.

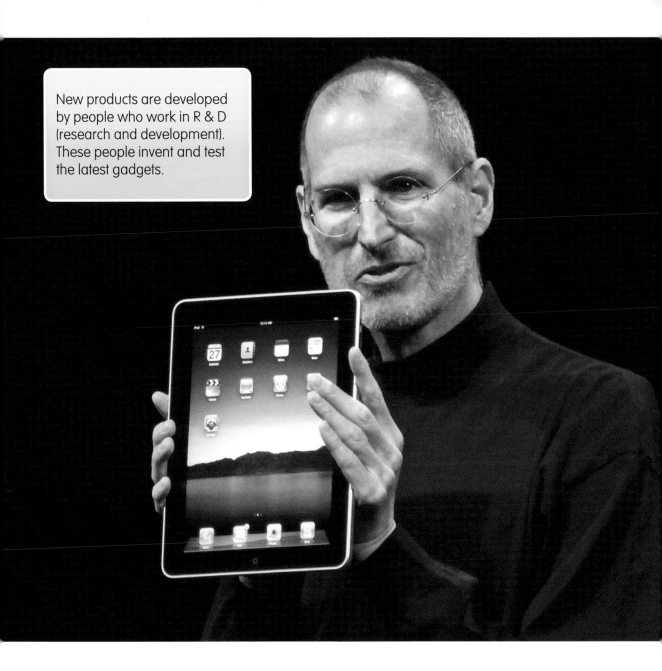

New products are developed by people who work in R & D (research and development). These people invent and test the latest gadgets.

Technology

Technology is not just important in **high-tech** industries. All areas of industry try to develop new technologies so they can make things more easily and cheaply. The way that people earn money has also changed because jobs that used to be done by people can now be done by computers.

Who works in services?

Most people in the modern economies of **developed countries** like the United States, Australia, the United Kingdom, and other European countries work in services. The total amount of **wealth** produced by a country is called the **Gross Domestic Product (GDP)** of that country. Much of the GDP of developed countries comes from services.

People who earn money in services do not make anything from **raw materials**. However, the economy could not function without the services they provide.

Think about the services you use every day. Your breakfast cereal probably came from a shop where people put it on the shelf and worked at the till. The driver who drove your bus to school provided a service. Your teacher at school is also providing a service, as are the doctors and nurses who would care for you if you were ill. There is a wide variety of people working in services. Some of them earn huge amounts of money every year; others earn very little.

Professions

If you are ill and go to see a doctor, you expect that doctor to be highly trained and know a lot about illness and how to cure it. Jobs such as doctors, lawyers, and teachers are sometimes called professions.

Doctors have to study for many years before they can call themselves a doctor. Because only the best students can become doctors, this and some other professions generally earn more money than jobs that do not require long training or special skills.

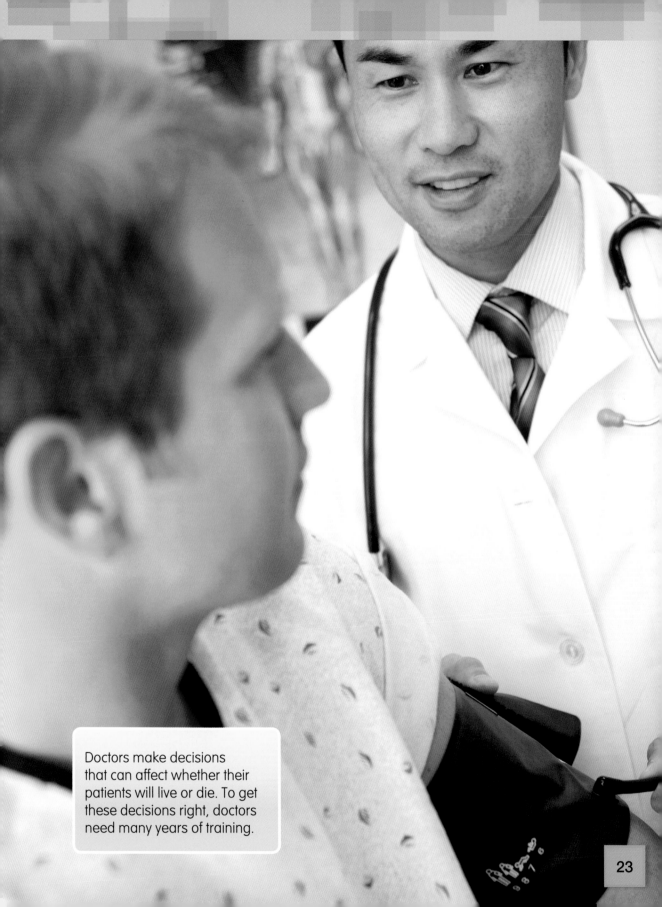

Doctors make decisions that can affect whether their patients will live or die. To get these decisions right, doctors need many years of training.

Banking and finance

One of the biggest service **industries** is banking and finance. Banks do more than give people a place to keep their money. They are important because they lend money to people to buy houses. Banks also lend money to businesses so they can **invest** more money to increase the size of the business. If companies have money to invest, they may expand their business and even hire more people.

This chart shows the proportion of people **employed** in different areas of the services sector.

| Hotels, restaurants and distribution including shops – 26% | Transport and communications – 3% | Banking and business – 21% | Education, health, and government – 43% |

Note: Other services account for 7 per cent.

Banks have been in the news a lot in the last few years. After making some bad business decisions, many banks have had to borrow money from the government to stay in business. Governments have supported banks because they fear that if the public lost complete faith in banks they would remove all of their money. Then, most of us would be unable to borrow money for cars, houses, or further education.

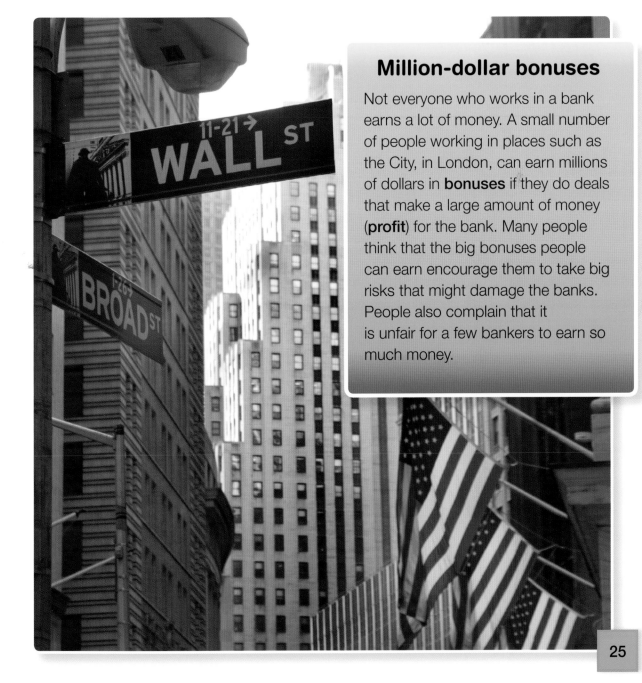

Million-dollar bonuses

Not everyone who works in a bank earns a lot of money. A small number of people working in places such as the City, in London, can earn millions of dollars in **bonuses** if they do deals that make a large amount of money (**profit**) for the bank. Many people think that the big bonuses people can earn encourage them to take big risks that might damage the banks. People also complain that it is unfair for a few bankers to earn so much money.

Greeting Cards

SUPPLIES

Cards

Books

ALWAYS Low Prices Always WAL·MART

2 for $5.00

SNACKS

Low Prices Always

$3.00

78

88

How 'bout a little Pepsi

PEPSI

Cheerios

Cheerios

POPS

POPS

PEPSI

01036 C

Kellogg's CORN POPS

01036 C

Kellogg's CORN POPS

01036 C

Kellogg's CORN POPS

The NEW

More people work for the US company Walmart than for any other private company. Asda in the UK is also part of Walmart.

Stores and restaurants

How many people work in your local shop? If it's a small shop, you might only see one person. There are many people who depend on shops to earn money. Bigger shops have buyers and managers who decide what the store will sell.

Hotels and restaurants also employ a lot of people. Those who work in hotels and restaurants often get very little pay. They expect to earn some money from tips. Customers will reward good service by paying a little extra for their meal.

Value of training

We saw earlier in this chapter that doctors are well paid because they are highly trained and have skills that are highly valued. Although there are many talented people working in shops and restaurants, unlike doctors, they do not have to train for many years. There are more people who could work in shops and restaurants so their **value**, or the amount they can earn, is lower.

Trade unions

For most people, earning money depends on finding a company that will pay them for their work. If the employer does not need you to work anymore, or they can find someone who will work for less money, you may lose your job. Many workers group together in trade unions to bargain with employers. A trade union has more power to bargain than a single worker, because it speaks for all the workers. The trade union can call a strike, meaning that all employees will stop work and the employer will be unable to run its business.

How do public sector workers earn money?

People who work for the local or national government are said to work in the public sector. These people include government officials, also called the civil service, and the armed forces. Most state school teachers are paid by the **Local Education Authority (LEA)** in which they work. In the United Kingdom, and many countries, the government also pays doctors and nurses.

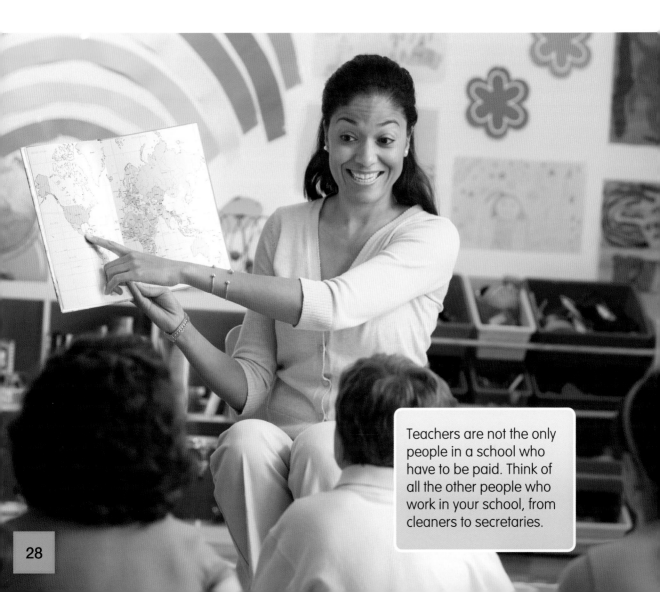

Teachers are not the only people in a school who have to be paid. Think of all the other people who work in your school, from cleaners to secretaries.

Paying taxes

The government can afford to pay all these people because everyone pays a proportion, or part, of what they earn to the government. This is called tax. Even workers who are paid by the government have to pay tax. We all pay tax whenever we buy something in a shop, because some of what we pay goes to the government in a tax called VAT (value added tax).

Government spending is normally a big point for discussion during elections. If people do not like the way their taxes are being spent, they will vote for a new government. **Politicians** often talk about cutting spending. Some of the spending is on paying people, so this often means that people will lose their jobs.

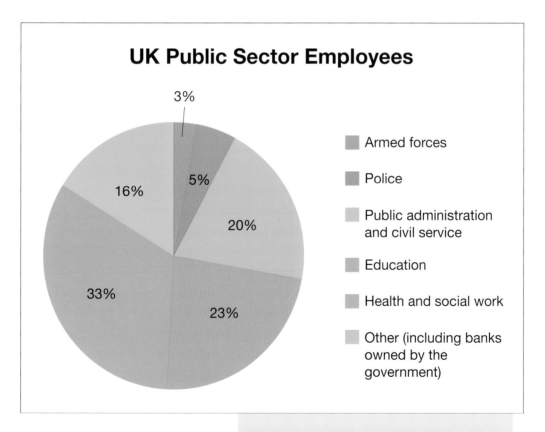

This pie chart shows the different jobs that are in the public sector. Areas where more people are employed will have a bigger section of the pie chart.

Does everyone work for someone else?

Not everyone earns money working for someone else. Many people start or run their own business. Most of these businesses are owned by a single person. They may have a particular skill, such as a plumber or electrician, or they may own a small shop. People who run their own business enjoy the freedom of not having to work for someone else. However, the success of the business and whether they get paid at the end of the month depends on them and whether their business makes a **profit**.

All businesses start small

Even though most of these businesses are very small, all of the world's major international companies were at one time small businesses. Bill Gates and Paul Allen started Microsoft when they left university in 1975. By the year 2000, it was one of the world's largest companies. Many other **high-tech** companies have grown dramatically in recent decades as the internet has changed many businesses.

Other ways to earn money include buying and selling property and **investing** in companies. These investments will hopefully rise in **value** over time. However, investments are risky and can lose value as well.

Madam C. J. Walker
(1867–1919)

Madam C.J. Walker became the first African-American woman millionaire in the United States. She was the daughter of former slaves. In 1905, she developed a product for straightening hair. Madam C. J. Walker's network of sales people sold her products across the United States. She once said "... if I have accomplished anything in life, it is because I have been willing to work hard."

Who decides how much people earn?

Although everyone needs to earn money, some people earn more than others. When you do paid work, you are basically selling your skill and the time you spend at work, just as if you were selling a product. The amount you are paid is your price, and this price is called a wage or salary. The amount you are paid will depend on how much people think your skills are worth.

Supply and demand

Wages, or the money earned from work, will be low for those jobs where there are many people who could do the job. Because there is a good supply of workers and the job does not require many special skills, employers do not have to pay high wages. The government sets a minimum wage that everyone should earn. Employers are not allowed to pay workers less than this amount.

The amount you can earn will rise if your skills are in high demand. This means that you have skills that are useful and cannot be easily found elsewhere. We have already discovered that doctors have skills that are in high demand.

Some jobs are particularly well paid because they require a talent that is in very short supply. Stars of sports, music, and entertainment are paid well because their talents are very rare.

Solve it!

Who earns more?
Which of these jobs do you think would be best paid? Why?

- supermarket worker

- bus driver

- lawyer

- football player

- plumber.

Airline pilots need many years of training. For this reason, the supply of airline pilots is limited and demand is high. This means that airline pilots have a high **value** to the companies they work for. But many airline pilots have received pay cuts because the airline industry has become less profitable in recent years.

What happens when people can't earn money?

At any time, there are a number of people in the economy who are not doing paid work. These people may have chosen not to work; they may stay at home to care for children or other family members. However, there are always people who would like to work but are unable to find a job. People who are not working but are looking for work are unemployed.

Unemployment

Television news reports often say that **unemployment** has risen or fallen. When unemployment increases, this means that more people have lost their jobs than have found new ones. People can lose their jobs for many different reasons.

Outsourcing

Companies may decide that they cannot afford to pay so many people to make and sell their products. They may also try to save money by employing a separate company who will do the same work for less money. This is called **outsourcing**. Many American and British companies have employed **call centres** in India to answer phone calls from customers in the United Kingdom and the United States.

Outsourcing call centres has been made possible by advances in phone technology. Changing technology is another reason why people lose their jobs. There are many examples of jobs that existed in history that are no longer needed. For example, when horses were the main means of road transport, every village had a **blacksmith**. Nowadays, only a few remain.

A computer on every desk is a recent technological development. Before the 1990s, companies employed many typists to type up letters and documents that are now produced on computers.

People who have retired hope that their pensions will earn them enough money to enjoy their retirement.

Benefits

When people lose their jobs, they can usually claim some money from the government to make sure they are able to pay for essentials such as housing and food. This money will only be enough to cover essential costs until they are able to find work again. **Benefits** are also available for anyone who is unable to work because of disability or long-term illness.

Retirement

Most of us don't want to work for our whole lives. People who have worked for many years normally retire, or stop working, in their sixties. Once they retire, they will earn no more money from work so they will need to have some money saved for retirement.

People save money for retirement in different ways. In the UK, most people receive a **pension** from the government. The amount of their pension is partly based on how much they have paid in **National Insurance contributions**. Public sector workers (people employed by the government) also receive a work-based pension from the local or national government when they retire. Many people pay money into a workplace pension scheme.

Other retirement income comes from money that people have saved throughout their working lives. They save this money into a scheme that **invests** the money in companies. Hopefully by the time they retire, the amount of money in the scheme will have increased.

Thinking about pensions

Do you save money to buy things you want? Maybe you have a bank account where you save money. Can you think of some reasons why it is a good idea to save money for the future?

Why does all this matter to me?

Hopefully this book will have given you more understanding of where money comes from and how it affects your family and friends. When you leave school or college, you will need to earn money of your own. We have seen that the economy is always changing. What are the opportunities going to be when you go to work?

Some ways of earning money have disappeared or changed dramatically; new jobs and **industries** will take their place. The growth of the internet has led to major changes in the economy since the 1990s. Emerging nations like China and India have become more important. Make sure you know what's happening so you can make informed choices about how you earn money.

Earning money now

It can be difficult for young people to earn money. There are many laws designed to protect young people, but these can limit your options.

- Sell things that you no longer need, either at a car boot sale or online. Make sure you get permission from an adult.

- Walk dogs for friends and family, or water plants and feed pets when family, friends, or neighbours are on holiday.

- Bake cakes and sell them at school or other events. Make sure that you have permission from the school.

Stay safe! Be very careful when dealing with strangers or meeting people online, who may not be who they say they are. Make sure an adult knows what you are doing and can go with you if you are meeting someone.

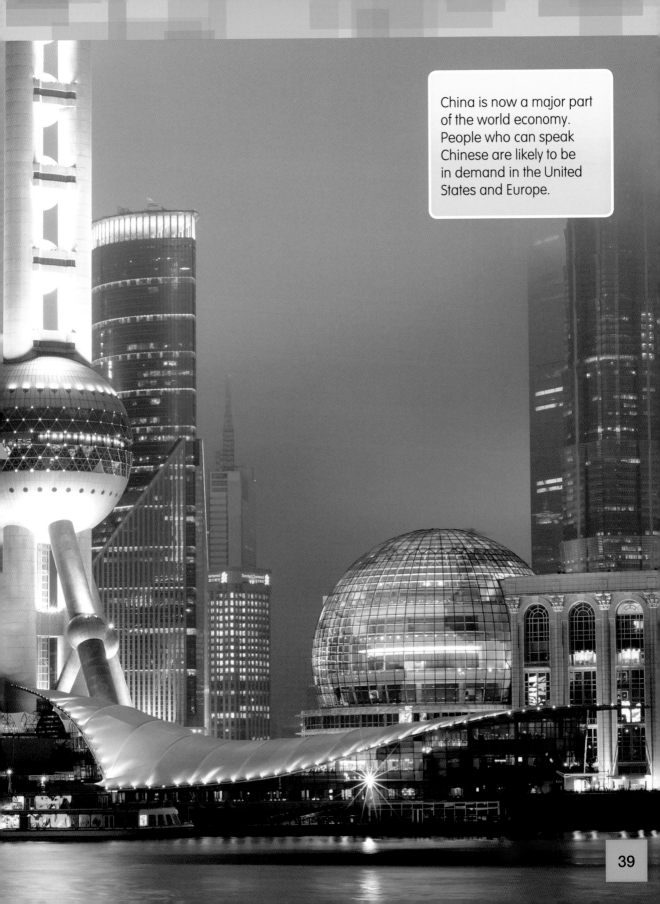

China is now a major part of the world economy. People who can speak Chinese are likely to be in demand in the United States and Europe.

How are you going to earn money?

When thinking about your own future career, you need to ask yourself a lot of questions. A rewarding career is not just about earning lots of money. There are many other things to consider.

Think about what you want to do and what you are good at. You might prefer to work outside, and this could lead you to a job in **agriculture**. You might want to follow a particular interest. Think about whether it is more important to you to earn lots of money or to do something that helps others.

Making the right choices and studying hard mean that you will have the most opportunities when you have to start earning money yourself.

Architects design structures, from small houses to skyscrapers and bridges. If you want to be an architect, you will need to study the right subjects at school and university.

People who work for charities do not usually earn a lot of money. However, helping others and doing a job you enjoy can be very rewarding.

Researching the world of work

There are many places where you can find out more about different ways of earning money. Your school or public library will have lots of information about different careers. If you are interested in a particular career, you may know someone who does that job already who can tell you more about it. Many companies are happy for young people to experience what it would be like to work there.

Who are the richest people in the world?

Carlos Slim

In March 2010, *Forbes* magazine named Mexican Carlos Slim as the world's richest man. Slim owns more than 200 companies, including Latin America's biggest mobile phone company. Despite his estimated fortune of $53.5 billion, he lives in a modest six-bedroom house. Inside, the walls of the house are covered with fantastic works of art.